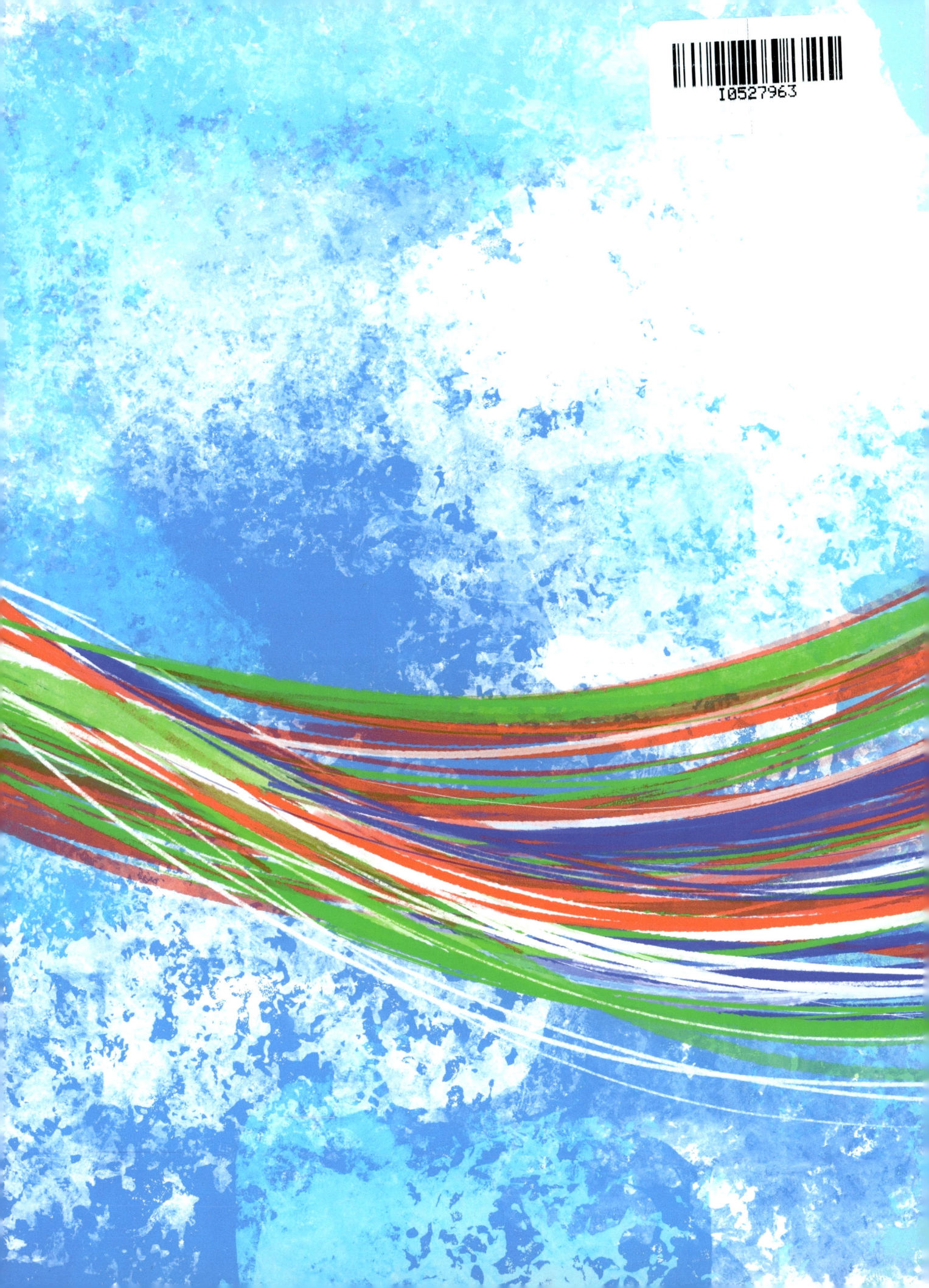

"Fernando's great for the Dodgers, great for baseball, great for the country—both of them [U.S. & Mexico]. No matter how hard life seems; kids can look up at him and say: He made it. So can I."

~Tommy Lasorda, legendary L.A. Dodger manager

To Dodgers fans everywhere!

~Kathleen Contreras

In memory of my younger brother Sahim Abraham Paniagua.

~Christian Paniagua

BORN TO PLAY BÉISBOL:
THE MAGICAL CAREER OF FERNANDO VALENZUELA

WRITTEN BY KATHLEEN CONTRERAS   ART BY CHRISTIAN PANIAGUA

ISBN: 979-8-9889541-0-1

Printed in the United States of America by IngramSpark.

Published in the United States of America
by Kathleen Contreras through Espejo Press.

Visit or contact us at
www.kathleencontreras.com

KATHLEEN
CONTRERAS

Fernando Valenzuela was born to play béisbol.

Growing up on a rancho in Sonora, Mexico, béisbol was a dirt field of dusty chalk marks for baselines.

Béisbol meant no plate nor backstop. It was logs for benches and a pitcher's mound made of an old wood pallet raised and topped with dirt. The field was simple, yet perfect, for chasing baseball dreams.

For Fernando, the youngest of twelve children, béisbol meant family and friends who nicknamed him... El Zurdo, a lefty pitcher.

Fernando lived with his big family in a small, but cozy adobe house with a wood stove, one light bulb, a metate stone for grinding corn for tortillas, and no running water.

Like a baseball team, his family worked together too. His siblings were his teammates and coaches. His oldest brother, Rafael, played Fernando on first base, sharpening his fielding skills, until he was 13, then switched him to pitching, where he blossomed.

As a teen, Fernando grew stronger and bigger until he was as fierce as a "toro," a strong bull. Later, El Toro would become his professional nickname. He was only 16, when he signed his first professional contract with a Mexican baseball team!

Now, béisbol meant traveling by bus with his teammates bouncing along curvy ribbons of roads across Mexico to play on fields surrounded by dark mountains, dry deserts, blue waters, and green jungles.

At each game, Fernando sharpened his arsenal of pitches: fastballs, sinkers, and curve balls. He was a fast learner, so his coaches taught him changeups and sliders too.

Three years and many innings later, a sharp-eyed Dodger scout, Mike Brito, flew to Mexico to discover new talent. As quick as a fast ball, he invited the teenage Fernando to play minor league baseball.

Fernando showed promise and later joined the Dodgers in the Major League, where a new teammate, Bobbie Castillo, taught him a new pitch ... the screwball.

Few batters could hit it. Even fewer pitchers could throw it, especially left-handed. This was it, a signature pitch! Fernando practiced and practiced, and soon mastered this crazy-style spiraling lefty pitch.

That screwball would change him and the game of baseball forever...

Fernando's major league debut was on baseball's favorite time of year...
Opening Day.

Players were excited for the new season--mitts were oiled, uniforms bright, balls tossed, and bats swung in lazy swings warming-up for the Houston Astros, on April 9, 1981. The smell of hotdogs filled the air and fans colored Dodger Stadium in blue and white baseball caps, shirts, and jerseys with the sounds of Helen Dell's organ playing "Take me Out to the Ballgame."

"It's time for Dodger baseball! "Lanzador, número #34, Fernando Valenzuela," announced Vin Scully and Jaime Jarrin, long-time veteran voices of the Dodgers.

Wait...Who? A rookie? On Opening Day?

Thousands of curious eyes watched Fernando warm-up, but 19-year-old Fernando seemed relaxed and confident. On his first pitch, Fernando winds up, kicks high, looks skyward, and throws a screwball.

What? A screwball?

"Who throws a screwball, especially left-handed?"
the batter and fans wonder.

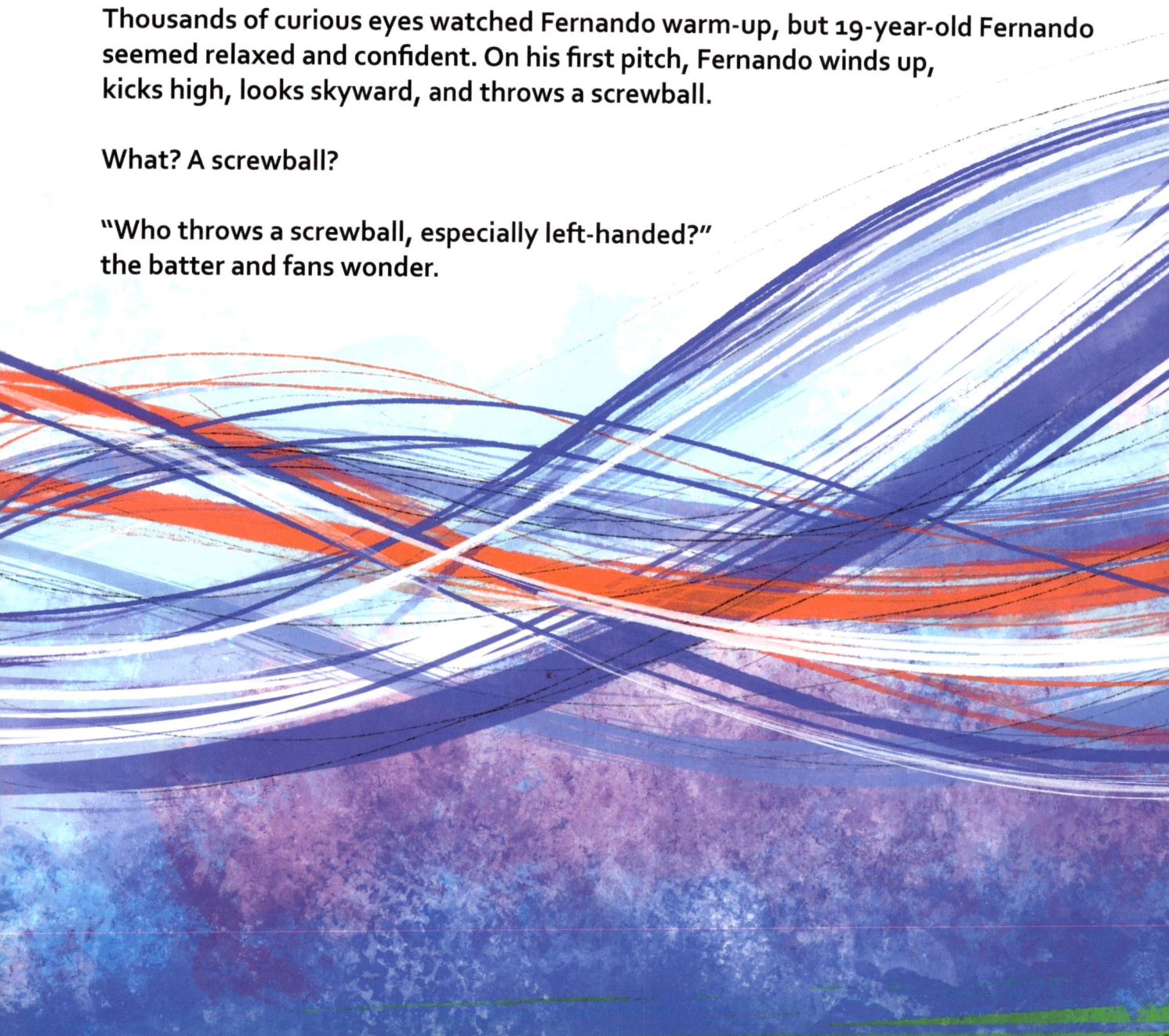

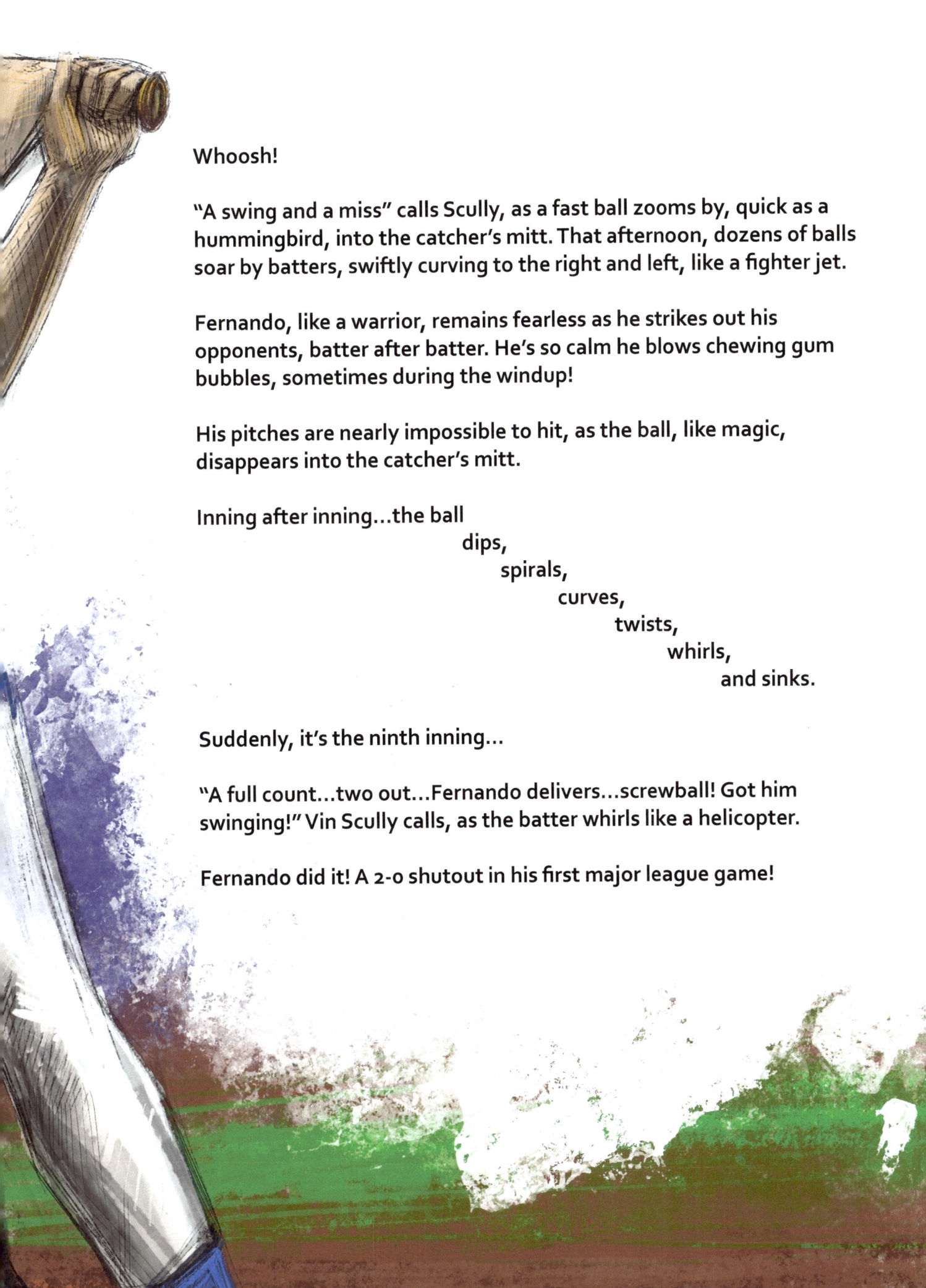

Whoosh!

"A swing and a miss" calls Scully, as a fast ball zooms by, quick as a hummingbird, into the catcher's mitt. That afternoon, dozens of balls soar by batters, swiftly curving to the right and left, like a fighter jet.

Fernando, like a warrior, remains fearless as he strikes out his opponents, batter after batter. He's so calm he blows chewing gum bubbles, sometimes during the windup!

His pitches are nearly impossible to hit, as the ball, like magic, disappears into the catcher's mitt.

Inning after inning...the ball
dips,
spirals,
curves,
twists,
whirls,
and sinks.

Suddenly, it's the ninth inning...

"A full count...two out...Fernando delivers...screwball! Got him swinging!" Vin Scully calls, as the batter whirls like a helicopter.

Fernando did it! A 2-0 shutout in his first major league game!

Over that entire rookie season, Fernando was magical on the mound… pitch after pitch, batter after batter, game after game.

Out of Dodger blue, Fernando became the most exciting pitcher to watch in all of baseball.

That rookie season, he led the entire league in wins, strikeouts, innings pitched, and shutouts! Fans witnessed the greatest start of a young pitcher in Major League baseball!

"He is nùmero #1 in the baseball world!" a sportswriter proclaims.

Thousands of his adoring fans, followed Fernando like a rock star, multiplying game after game, waving homemade signs:

¡Viva Fernando! El Toro Forever! We love Fernando!

And U.S. and Mexico flags flew proudly at stadiums, on cars, at homes, and around neighborhoods.

This feverish time was called, Fernandomania, as fans, players, and sports writers went crazy over the young man from a rancho in Mexico. It spread like wildfire, igniting not only Dodger Stadium, but selling out every ballpark across the country, from Yankee Stadium to Wrigley Field, down to Miami, building fans across the nation, and north to Montreal, Canada!

Everyone wanted a chance to see El Toro, their superhero, in action!

"He's one of us," said a Latino fan. "Fernando's familia, he looks like us and speaks our language."

Hundreds of vendors lined the streets leading to Dodger stadium in Chavez Ravine, selling Fernando's trading cards, posters, and T-shirts. Spanish and English echoed in the air, while mariachis serenaded fans with violins plucking, guitars strumming, horns blaring, and gritos shouting!

More than a sporting event, Fernandomania became a party, a fiesta where more than béisbol was spoken.

But baseball wasn't all party for Fernando…

"Going to a different country, with a new language and traditions was going to be difficult. I didn't know what was going to happen," reflected Fernando.

"I wondered how I would get used to a new way of life," said Fernando, who practiced English by watching television and playing jokes on his teammates. He even eased game time jitters, making lassos with a short rope, tripping teammates in the dugout!

But mostly, Fernando let his pitching do the talking, especially with catcher, Mike Scioscia. Fernando and Mike were a team within a team—the pitcher and catcher. The ball and mitt—two opposites, they connected like a magnet.

And Fernando wasn't a one season star. Almost ten years after Fernandomania, he pitched one of his greatest games...

--a no-hitter against the St. Louis Cardinals in June 1990!

"If you have a sombrero, throw it to the sky!" called Scully, on the last pitch, to thousands of cheering fans, across the city, around the country, and beyond the border.

Fans shouted... "¡Fer...nan...do! "¡Viva Valenzuela!

"How do you feel Fernando, pitching a no-hitter?" asked a sportswriter.

"Honestly, beside pitching in the World Series, building a new house for my parents, is the proudest moment for me," said a modest Fernando, who thought of his family, as his "home" team.

Fernando and Fernandomania brought more to baseball than his left-handed screwball; they created thousands of new fans to L.A. and to ballparks across the nation. And global players from the Americas, the Caribbean, and Asia continue to migrate to Major League baseball through the door Fernando helped opened.

That young boy from a small rancho in Mexico, grew up to be a legend in one of America's biggest sports cities.

Whatever you call it, béisbol or baseball, Fernando Valenzuela, was born to play the game.

Author's Note

Fernando contributed much more to baseball than his left-handed screwball. He brought thousands of fans, new and old, to stadiums across the country. Legendary commentator Jaime Jarrín confirmed the increase in attendance:

"I truly believe that there is no other player in the history of the Major Leagues who has created more new fans than Fernando Valenzuela, Sandy Koufax, Don Drysdale, Joe DiMaggio, not even Babe Ruth. Fernando made fans of many people from Mexico, Central America and South America. It created interest in baseball among people who didn't care about baseball."

Fernando and Fernandomania sparked not only fans, but also other Latino and Asian players to play on baseball fields in the United States. Now, all teams in the national and American leagues have players from all over the world, who speak their native languages and the language of baseball.

Like the Statue of Liberty, Fernando's success welcomed everyone to America's favorite game. Players from the Dominican Republic, Mexico, Cuba, Puerto Rico, Panama, Venezuela, Japan and Korea come to play on the baseball fields of the United States, expanding the boundaries of Major League Baseball.

The years Fernando spent playing baseball at Dodger Stadium in Chavez Ravine also brought back memories of a displaced community, with echoes of Spanish and English spoken all around the city of Los Angeles. Now, his fandom includes all Angelenos, especially Latinos.

Currently, Fernando broadcasts live Dodger action on television in Spanish and supports Dodger community events. His beloved #34 jersey is officially retired (as of August 11, 2023). Fernando is now an American citizen, a member of the illustrious Dodger Legends, a member of the California Hall of Fame, and an owner of a Mexican baseball team. He's a family man: a husband, father of four children, and grandfather.

Fernando showed that the American dream can be achieved by everyone who lives in America, not just those born in the US. Like so many others who cross borders, Fernando lives comfortably crossing between the US and Mexico, embodying the American dream.

~Kathleen Contreras

1 Jorge Martin, "25 Years After Fernandomania," Dodger Magazine, 18 August 2006.

The Stats

Fernando's baseball career began in the Mexican Baseball league when he was 16 years old. In 1977, Valenzuela began his professional baseball career when he signed with the Mayos de Navojoa. A year later, he was sent to the Guanajuato Tuzos, and later played with the Leones de Yucatan.

His U.S. professional career debut at 19 years old, ignited the L.A. Dodgers franchise, where he pitched 11 seasons and 141 games (8th in franchise history) from 1980-1990.

In his rookie season, Fernando Valenzuela won his first eight starts (five shutouts!). He became the only player in Major League history to win the Rookie of the Year Award, the Cy Young Award for Best Pitcher in the same season, and the National League Silver Slugger Award for Best Pitcher. In his rookie year, Fernando's 11 of out 12 starts pitching at Dodger Stadium were sellouts!

From 1981 to 1987, Fernando won more games than any other National League starter and had the second-best ERA of NL pitchers with 1,000 innings. Fernando also completed more games in Dodger history since Sandy Koufax in 1966, winning 21 games, completing 20. In 1986, one of his best seasons, he finished 21-11 with 3.14 ERA and led the league in wins, complete games, and innings pitched.

Fernando was also a team member of the Dodger's 1986 World Series team. He was named a six-time All Star (1981–1986) and was known to be one of the best hitting pitchers, winning the national league's Silver Slugger award twice for pitchers.

Fernando played 17-years in Major League baseball, playing until 1997. Playing for six different professional teams, he achieved his greatest success with the Dodgers, where he currently does play-by-play Spanish language broadcasting for Spectrum SportsNet TV.

In 2019, the Mexican baseball league retired Fernando's #34 for all Mexican teams. The Los Angeles Dodgers honored Fernando by officially retiring #34 jersey on August 11, 2023.

Dr. Kathleen Contreras is a bilingual educator teaching in both public and private universities in California.

She is the author of five bilingual children's books: Pan Dulce (Scholastic); Braids/Trencitas (Lectorum Publications); Sweet Memories/Dulces Recuerdos (Lectorum); Harvesting Friends/Cosechando Amigos (Arte Público Press) and Born to Play Béisbol: The Magical Career of Fernando Valenzuela (Espejo Press).

kathleencontreras.com

Christian Paniagua, a native New Yorker, is a seasoned illustrator and graphic design artist with a rich 25-year career. A proud alumnus of Pratt Institute, he holds two degrees in Communication Design, showcasing his dedication to honing his craft. Christian's artistic journey is deeply rooted in his urban upbringing, intertwined with a genuine passion for animation and comics.

His unique artistic signature is a whimsical blend of movement, vibrant colors, and evocative emotions, reflecting the dynamic essence of his urban roots. Christian's ability to infuse these elements into his artwork provides him the freedom to diversify his designs across various themes and genres. His illustrious career stands as a testament to his proficiency and creativity in the realm of children's book illustration, captivating audiences with each stroke of his imaginative brush.